Maths Problem-Solving

5-7 years

Notes for grown-ups

● This book has been written to help your child develop their first maths skills. They will practise maths problem-solving and addition, multiplication and division, using patterns, measurements and number sequences.

● The activities in this book are organized to build on what your child learned on the previous page. If they are finding something tricky, go back to a page they feel confident with.

● Some of the activities in this book require additional learning materials. You will need some coloured pencils or crayons, tape, paper, string, and a tape measure or a ruler.

● Left-handed children should tilt the book so that the top left corner is higher than the right. The book should be slightly to the left of their bodies. This will help them to see their writing and avoid smudging.

● Look out for the **How are you doing?** sections. These give your child an opportunity to reflect on their progress and give you an idea of how your child is doing.

● Let your child check their own answers at the back of the book. Encourage them to talk about what they have learned.

Educational Consultant: Claire Hubbard.
With thanks to Child Autism UK, Pace, Amy Callaby and Jack Callaby.

Your Ladybird Class friends!

Zara Penguin loves all kinds of dance, as well as stories about princesses, knights and superheroes. Zara has cerebral palsy and wears an ankle-foot orthosis on each leg to help her walk. Her favourite lessons are history and circle time.

Nia Hedgehog is the newest member of Ladybird Class! She loves video games and skateboarding. Her favourite lessons are computing and geography.

Tao Meerkat wants to save the planet! He loves animals, nature and the environment. But he also likes magical stories and role-playing. His favourite lessons are science and phonics.

Olivia Crocodile always has lots of energy and is ready to change the world! She loves building things, and she has a red belt in karate. Her favourite lessons are maths and PE.

Noah Panda loves to craft, play on the computer and, most of all, he loves to bake. He collects lots of things like badges and pebbles. Noah is on the autism spectrum. His favourite lessons are art and playtime.

Ali Lion is quiet, but his head is full of daydreams and imagination. He loves to sing and to dress up in fancy costumes. His favourite lessons are literacy and music.

Contents

Bowling scores

Ladybird Class are on a bowling trip! Can you use your adding-up skills to work out their scores?

How to play

In this game, there are 10 skittles. Ladybird Class are rolling a ball at the skittles to knock them down! They all get 2 tries at rolling the ball, and the fallen skittles are cleared away after each go.

Olivia Crocodile's turn

Nia Hedgehog's turn

Zara Penguin's turn

Ali Lion's turn

Noah Panda's turn

Let's write the results on a scoreboard! How many skittles were knocked down on each player's first try, and on their second try? How many skittles did each player knock down in total?

Who knocked the most skittles down?

Player	First try	Second try	Total
Olivia	5	1	6

The garden centre

Ladybird Class are choosing plants for their new school garden.
Use your number skills to help them out!

Flower plants

Can you help me choose 20 flower plants, please? I want some of each kind of flower.

Flower plants:
20 for £5

Write down what you think Noah Panda should choose.

[ ] + [ ] + [ ] = 20 flower plants

Lettuce plants

Lettuce plants: Trays of 6

I need 18 lettuce plants. How many trays do I need to buy?

[ ] lots of 6 = 18

[ ] × 6 = 18

Nia Hedgehog needs to buy [ ] trays of lettuce plants.

Daffodil bulbs

I need to share the daffodil bulbs equally between 5 flowerbeds.

1 — 36 bulbs

2 — 48 bulbs

3 — 60 bulbs

The number of daffodil bulbs that will share equally between 5 is ☐ .

Olivia Crocodile should buy bag ☐ .

Tomato plants

I can buy 3 tomato plants with £1. How many can I buy for £5?

5 lots of 3 = ☐

5 × 3 = ☐

Tomato plants: 3 for £1

Ali Lion can buy ☐ tomato plants for £5.

A treasure map

Ladybird Class have found an old treasure map! It is marked into 100 squares. Use your maths skills to answer the questions.

1	2	3	4	5	6	7	8	9	10
11	12	13	14	15	16	17	18	19	20
	22	23	24	25	26	27	28	29	30
31	32	33	34	35	36	37	38	39	
41	42	43	44	45	46	47	48	49	50
51	52	53	54	55	56		58	59	60
61	62	63	64	65	66	67	68	69	70
71		73	74	75	76	77	78	79	80
81	82	83	84	85	86	87	88	89	90
91	92	93	94	95	96	97	98	99	100

Use the map to answer these questions and find the pictures.

What is . . .	Number	Picture
9 less than 46?		
4 more than 22?		
6 less than 49?		
8 more than 63?		

Which numbers are missing from the map?

Your treasure hunt

Think of some more questions you could ask about the treasure map. You could even draw some more things to find.

What is . . .	Number	Picture

How are you doing?

How are you feeling about finding your way around a 100 square?

- [ ] I feel great! I can't wait to draw a 100 square map to play with.
- [ ] I'm getting there, but I'd like to practise some more.

The magic show

Tao Meerkat is practising some new magic tricks. But he's making a few mistakes. Can you help Tao improve his tricks?

Disappearing numbers

Can you see the magic numbers on my handkerchiefs? They add up to 10.

No, they don't!

3 1 1 2 2 3

Which 5 numbers should stay? They must add up to 10.

☐ + ☐ + ☐ + ☐ + ☐ = 10

The number ☐ should disappear.

Here are some more numbers. I'll try to count correctly this time. They add up to 20!

They don't! Check again!

5 1 3 3 6 7

Which 5 numbers should stay?

☐ + ☐ + ☐ + ☐ + ☐ = 20

The number ☐ should disappear.

Disappearing rabbits

And now, for my next trick! My performing rabbits will line up to count in 2s. Can you count them?

2 4 8 10 14 16 20

Which numbers are missing? Write the correct line of numbers here.

2 ☐ ☐ ☐ ☐ ☐ ☐ ☐ ☐ ☐

Let me try again. Now my performing rabbits will count in 5s. Count them all!

5 10 15 20 30 35 40 50

Which numbers are missing? Write the correct line of numbers here.

5 ☐ ☐ ☐ ☐ ☐ ☐ ☐ ☐ ☐

The rabbits keep jumping away!

11

The party

Ladybird Class are preparing for a class party. But the friends have some maths problems to solve first.

Cutting the sandwiches

I have cut this sandwich into 2 rectangles. They are both the same shape and size.

How can we cut my sandwich so that we have 2 triangles? Draw a line where you would cut it.

Now let's cut 4 triangles. You will need to draw 2 lines this time.

Now let's cut 4 squares. You will need to draw 2 lines again.

Now cut 4 long, thin sandwiches, like fingers. You will need to draw 3 lines.

You can cut this one however you like. What shape will you choose?

Decorating the cake

Use coloured pens or crayons to decorate the cake with a repeating pattern. Use one of the examples or make up your own.

I've got some ideas for patterns and decorations here.

Making party bags

It's time to make your own party bag. You can choose any of these things, but you cannot spend more than 20p.

Which things will you put in the party bag? Draw them in the bag below.

Party blower 3p

Balloon 2p

Pot of bubbles 7p

Pencil 3p

Packet of raisins 5p

Whistle 10p

The nature reserve

Tao Meerkat is in a nature reserve quietly watching the animals. Can you help Tao to keep a record of what he sees?

Tao's tallies

Every time I see an animal, I draw a line next to its picture. I draw straight lines all the way up to four. When I get to five, I draw a line across the other four lines. This makes counting in 5s easier!

squirrel	HHH
bird	I
frog	II
fish	
bird	
mouse	
duck	
butterfly	

Animal chart

Tao saw 5 squirrels, so he has coloured in 5 squares above the squirrel. This is called a block graph. Can you use your tallies to complete this block graph? Choose a different colour for each animal.

5								
4								
3								
2								
1								

Which animal did Tao see most of? _____

Baking day

Noah Panda and Olivia Crocodile are baking fairy cakes. Can you help them to follow the recipe?

Weighing the ingredients

To make 6 fairy cakes, they will need:

50 grams of butter
50 grams of sugar
1 egg
50 grams of flour

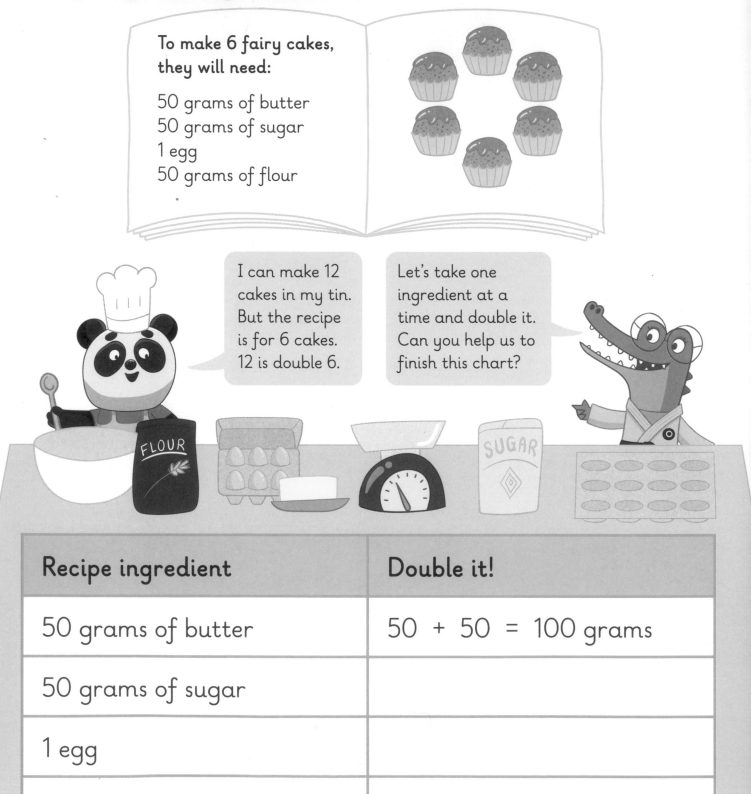

I can make 12 cakes in my tin. But the recipe is for 6 cakes. 12 is double 6.

Let's take one ingredient at a time and double it. Can you help us to finish this chart?

Recipe ingredient	Double it!
50 grams of butter	50 + 50 = 100 grams
50 grams of sugar	
1 egg	
50 grams of flour	

*Recipe for illustrative purposes only

Turning on the oven

Olivia Crocodile has asked a grown-up to help turn the oven on. The oven temperature must be 180 degrees celsius.

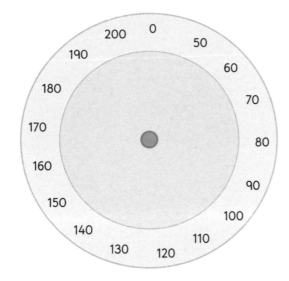

Circle 180 on the oven, then draw a dial pointing to 180. Now the oven is at the right temperature to bake our cakes!

Counting paper cases

I only have 4 paper cases, Olivia. How many more do we need to get to 12?

Start on 4. How many jumps does it take you to get to 12?

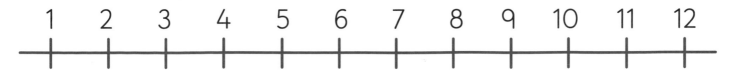

Now can you complete this number sentence?

4 + ☐ = 12   We need ☐ more paper cases.

The ice-cream queue

Ladybird Class are visiting the park. It's a hot day, so lots of customers are queuing up for ice creams.

| 1st | 2nd | 3rd | 4th | 5th | 6th | 7th |

1   2   3   4   5   6   7

The customer at the front is ⬜ **1st** in the queue.

Noah Panda is ⬜ in the queue.

Zara Penguin is ⬜ in the queue.

Olivia Crocodile is ⬜ in the queue.

Nia Hedgehog is ⬜ in the queue.

Tao Meerkat is ⬜ in the queue.

What is the 6th customer holding? _____

Ordinal numbers are numbers like **first (1st)**, **second (2nd)**, **third (3rd)**, **fourth (4th)**, and so on. We use ordinal numbers to order and position things, like all of these customers in the ice-cream queue!

What is the 9th customer holding? _____

Draw a hat on the 3rd customer.

Draw some shoes on the 8th customer.

Draw some glasses on the 11th customer.

Draw a scarf on the 13th customer.

Draw a walking stick for the 14th customer.

When the 1st customer leaves, who will be 1st in the queue?

_____

In the cafe

Ladybird Class are going to buy their lunch at the cafe today.

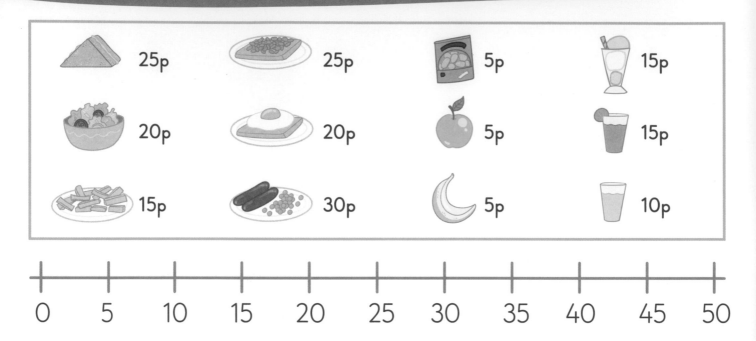

sandwich 25p	beans 25p	crisps 5p	milkshake 15p
salad 20p	egg 20p	apple 5p	juice 15p
chips 15p	sausages 30p	banana 5p	water 10p

```
+---+---+---+---+---+---+---+---+---+---+---+
0   5   10  15  20  25  30  35  40  45  50
```

Each of the friends has 50p to spend in the cafe.
Can you use the number line to help them add up their bills?

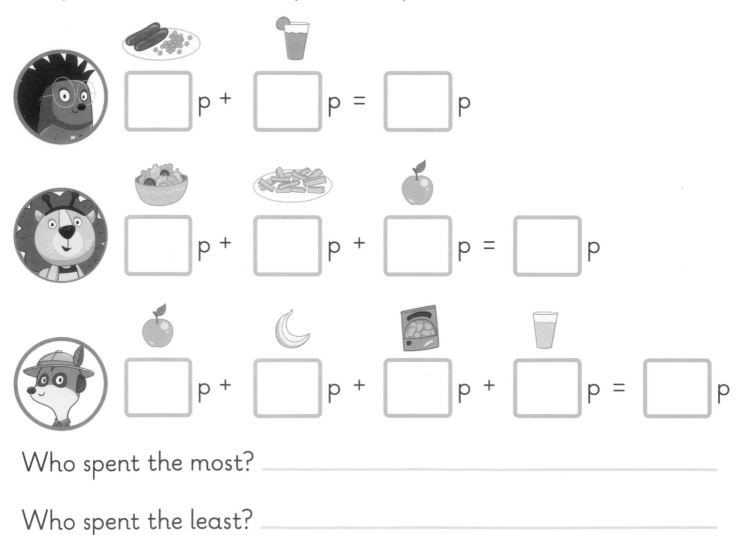

☐ p + ☐ p = ☐ p

☐ p + ☐ p + ☐ p = ☐ p

☐ p + ☐ p + ☐ p + ☐ p = ☐ p

Who spent the most? _____

Who spent the least? _____

Working out the change

Now work out how much change they will each get from 50p. You can use the number line to help. Start on 50, then count back in 5s.

Nia Hedgehog spent ☐ p.   50p − ☐ p = ☐ p

Nia spent   Nia's change

Nia will get ☐ p change.

Ali Lion spent ☐ p.

50p − ☐ p = ☐ p

Ali spent   Ali's change

Ali will get ☐ p change.

Tao Meerkat spent ☐ p.

50p − ☐ p = ☐ p

Tao spent   Tao's change

Tao will get ☐ p change.

Pretend you have 50p. What would you choose at the cafe? How much would you spend? How much change would you get?

How are you doing?

You've been adding and subtracting with money. How do you feel?

☐ I feel great! I can add and subtract with money and find the change.
☐ I would like some more help with this, please.

Party outfits

It's time for a class party! Practise using measure and pattern to help the friends make colourful hats and jewellery.

Zara Penguin and Tao Meerkat are making party hats.
But the paper strip is a little too long for Zara's head!

First, we wrap the string around your head, Zara, and let it overlap a little bit. I put my finger where the string needs to be cut. The string now tells us what size the hat should be.

Then, we put the string along the paper so we know where to cut.

That's perfect! Now I can decorate it.

Another way to measure is to use a tape measure. Can you see the numbers on the tape measure? Each numbered space on the tape measure is 1 centimetre.

1 2 3 4 5 6 7 8 9 10 11 12 13 14 15 16 17 18 19

Try measuring things with this tape measure! Can you find something that is 1 centimetre long? How about 5 centimetres?

Now measure round your head with a real tape measure.

What size is it? _____ centimetres

We're making necklaces out of colourful pasta to wear at the party!

Count how many pieces of pasta Ali Lion has used.

☐ orange pieces

☐ blue pieces

☐ pieces altogether

Noah Panda has made a necklace with a colour pattern. Can you work out what colours come next? Colour in the next 3 pieces of pasta in the pattern.

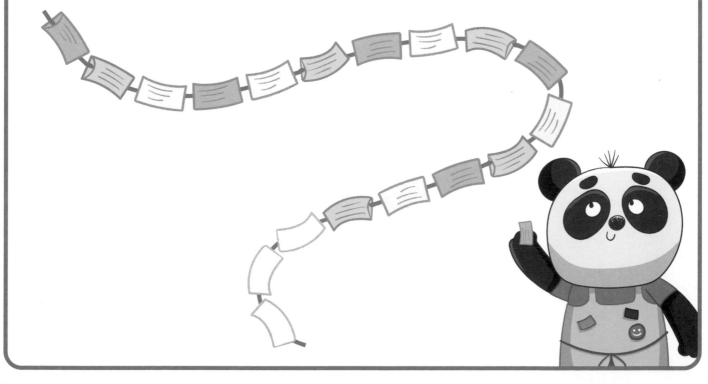

The safari park

It's an exciting day for Ladybird Class. They're visiting a safari park! Help them count, halve and double the number of animals they see.

Count the number of animals in the safari park and write your answers in the boxes.

☐ zebras   ☐ monkeys

☐ giraffes   ☐ elephants

After lunch, some of the animals went inside and some others came out to play. Fill in the table to show how many animals there are. Then draw them in the safari park.

Instructions	Number of animals
Draw double the number of zebras.	
Draw half the number of monkeys.	
Draw half the number of giraffes.	
Draw double the number of elephants.	

Hide-and-seek

Can you play hide-and-seek with Ladybird Class?
You will need to describe some places and positions!

We are playing hide-and-seek!
I must count to 20 before I
can go and look for the others.

Count to 20 with Zara Penguin, then describe where each person is hiding.
You will find some words to help you at the top of the page.

Noah Panda is _____ that tree.

Tao Meerkat is _____ the tunnel.

Ali Lion is _____ that bush.

Olivia Crocodile is _____ the little hill.

Nia Hedgehog is _____ those trees.

between   behind   above   under

in front of   inside   beside   on top of

Now it's Nia's turn to seek.
Where are you going to hide?
Draw a picture of your
hiding place.

My hiding place is _____ .

The computer maze

Ladybird Class are playing a computer game. Everyone needs to guide their game character through a maze to find a piece of fruit.

How to play

Follow the directions to take each character to a fruit. Remember to stay on the same square when you turn.

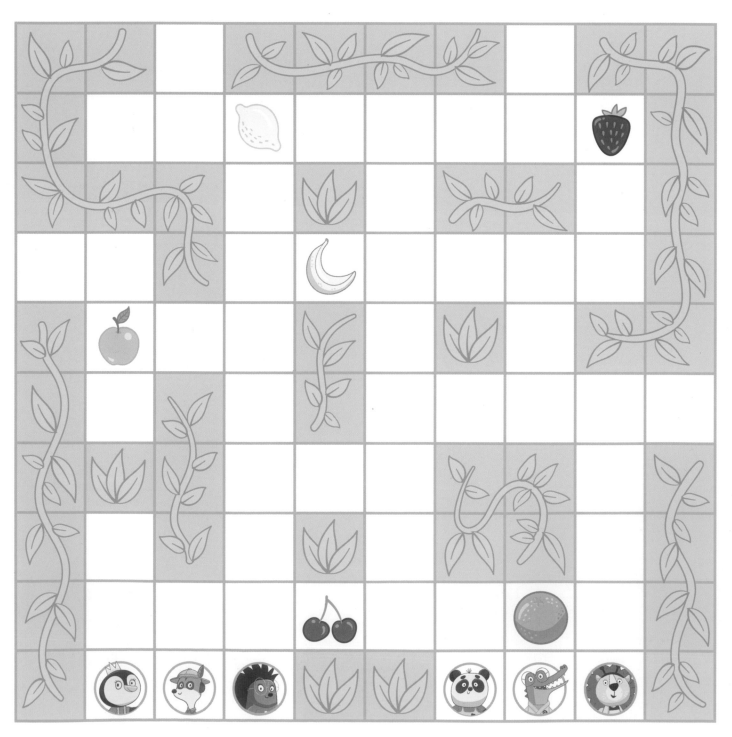

Go forward 1 square.
Turn right.
Go forward 2 squares.
Turn left.
Go forward 4 squares.
Turn left.
Go forward 2 squares.

Zara Penguin is now on the

_____ .

Go forward 1 square.
Turn right.
Go forward 1 square.

Noah Panda is now on the

_____ .

Go forward 1 square.
Turn right.
Go forward 1 square.
Turn left.
Go forward 7 squares.

Tao Meerket is now on the

_____ .

Go forward 1 square.
Turn left.
Go forward 3 squares.

Olivia Crocodile is now on

the _____ .

Go forward 8 squares.
Turn right.
Go forward 5 squares.

Nia Hedgehog is now on the

_____ .

Go forward 4 squares.
Turn left.
Go forward 3 squares.
Turn right.
Go forward 2 squares.
Turn left.
Go forward 1 square.

Ali Lion is now on the

_____ .

How are you doing?

How are you feeling about giving directions using numbers?

☐ I feel confident. I could show my friend how to play this game.

☐ I'm getting there, but it's a bit tricky. I'd like more help.

Crossing the swamp

Ali Lion, Nia Hedgehog and Zara Penguin need to cross the swamp to reach their friends on the other side. Can you help them find a path by solving the clues?

Start
What is double 7, take away 9?

Start
Add the number of legs on a spider to the number of wings on a fly.

Start
Take the number of legs on an insect from the number of days in a week.

10
What is 2 times 5, take away 8?

15
There are 14 ears on some donkeys. How many donkeys are there?

5
If there are 6 heads, how many eyes are there?

2
How many legs do 3 flamingos have altogether?

1
How many sides are there on 5 triangles?

12
Add the number of legs on a horse to the number of wings on 2 birds.

6

How many sides are there on a square?

9

What is 2 more than a dozen?

7

Take 3 from the number of months in a year.

13

What is half of the largest number you can throw on a dice?

4

There are 4 bicycles and a tricycle. How many wheels are there?

8

Add the number of legs on 3 dogs to the number of tails on a piglet.

3

14

11

Answers

Pages 4–5
Bowling scores

Nia Hedgehog	2	4	2 + 4 = 6
Zara Penguin	0	7	0 + 7 = 7
Ali Lion	7	2	7 + 2 = 9
Noah Panda	10	0	10 + 0 = 10

Noah knocked the most skittles down.

Pages 6–7
The garden centre
Flower plants
There are many different combinations of plants that will make 20. Ask a grown-up to check your answer.
Lettuce plants
3 lots of 6 = 18
3 × 6 = 18
Nia Hedgehog needs to buy 3 trays of lettuce plants.
Daffodil bulbs
The number of daffodil bulbs that will share equally between 5 is 60.
Olivia Crocodile should buy bag 3.
Tomato plants
5 lots of 3 = 15
5 × 3 = 15
Ali Lion can buy 15 tomato plants for £5.

Pages 8–9
A treasure map
9 less than 46
= square: 37 / picture: crab
4 more than 22
= square: 26 / picture: jewel
6 less than 49
= square: 43 / picture: chest
8 more than 63
= square: 71 / picture: volcano
The missing numbers are 21, 40, 57, 72.

Pages 10–11
The magic show
Disappearing numbers
3 + 1 + 1 + 2 + 3 = 10
The number 2 should disappear.
1 + 3 + 3 + 6 + 7 = 20
The number 5 should disappear.
Disappearing rabbits
2s: 2, 4, 6, 8, 10, 12, 14, 16, 18, 20
5s: 5, 10, 15, 20, 25, 30, 35, 40, 45, 50

Pages 12–13
The party
Cutting the sandwiches

2 triangles: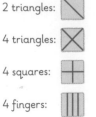

4 triangles:

4 squares:

4 fingers:

Making party bags
There are many different ways to spend 20p or less. Ask a grown-up to check your answer.

Pages 14–15
The nature reserve
Tao's tallies

Squirrels	5	ЦHT
Robins	1	|
Frogs	2	||
Fish	3	|||
Bluebirds	2	||
Mice	1	|
Ducks	1	|
Butterflies	4	||||

Animal chart

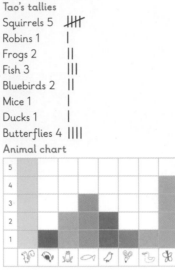

Tao Meerkat saw the most squirrels.

Pages 16–17
Baking day
Weighing the ingredients
50 + 50 = 100 grams of sugar
1 + 1 = 2 eggs
50 + 50 = 100 grams of flour
Turning on the oven

Finding paper cases
4 + 8 = 12
We need 8 more paper cases.

Pages 18–19
The ice-cream queue
Noah Panda is 2nd in the queue.
Zara Penguin is 5th in the queue.
Olivia Crocodile is 7th in the queue.
Nia Hedgehog is 10th in the queue.
Tao Meerkat is 12th in the queue.
The 6th customer is holding a football.
The 9th customer is holding a toy.
Noah Panda will be 1st in the queue.

Pages 20–21
In the cafe
Lunch orders
Nia Hedgehog: 30p + 15p = 45p
Ali Lion: 20p + 15p + 5p = 40p
Tao Meerkat: 5p + 5p + 5p + 10p = 25p
Nia Hedgehog spent the most.
Tao Meerkat spent the least.
Working out the change
Nia Hedgehog spent 45p.
50p – 45p = 5p
Nia will get 5p change.
Ali Lion spent 40p.

50p – 40p = 10p
Ali will get 10p change.
Tao Meerkat spent 25p.
50p – 25p = 25p
Tao will get 25p change.

Pages 22–23
Party outfits

4 orange pieces
6 blue pieces
10 pieces altogether

Pages 24–25
The safari park
3 zebras, 10 monkeys, 4 giraffes, 2 elephants
Double 3 zebras is 6 zebras.
Half of 10 monkeys is 5 monkeys.
Half of 4 giraffes is 2 giraffes.
Double 2 elephants is 4 elephants.
Ask a grown-up to check you have drawn the correct number of animals.

Pages 26–27
Hide-and-seek
Noah Panda is behind that tree.
Tao Meerkat is inside the tunnel.
Ali Lion is under that bush.
Olivia Crocodile is on top of the little hill.
Nia Hedgehog is between those trees.

Pages 28–29
The computer maze
Zara Penguin: apple; Tao Meerkat: lemon; Nia Hedgehog: strawberry; Noah Panda: orange; Olivia Crocodile: cherries; Ali Lion: banana

Pages 30–31
Crossing the swamp
Ali Lion's path
Double 7 take away 9 is 5.
There are 12 eyes on 6 heads.
4 legs on a horse + 2 wings on a bird + 2 wings on a bird = 8
4 legs on a dog + 4 legs on a dog + 4 legs on a dog + 1 tail on a piglet = 13
3 is half of the largest number you can throw on a dice.
Ali Lion will meet Olivia Crocodile.
Nia Hedgehog's path
8 legs on a spider + 2 wings on a fly = 10
2 times 5 = 10 – 8 = 2
3 flamingos × 2 legs on each flamingo = 6 legs
Squares have 4 sides.
2 wheels on a bicycle × 4 = 8 wheels; 8 bicycle wheels + 3 tricycle wheels = 11 wheels
Nia Hedgehog will meet Tao Meerkat.
Zara Penguin's path
7 days in a week – 6 legs on an insect = 1
There are 3 sides on 1 triangle, so 15 sides on 5 triangles.
There are 2 ears on each donkey. 14 ears ÷ 2 ears per donkey = 7 donkeys
12 months in the year – 3 = 9
A dozen is 12. 12 + 2 = 14
Zara Penguin will meet Noah Panda.